The HTML5 Dictionary

The HTML5 Dictionary

Compiled by
Mark Lassoff

ISBN: 9798398206937

Framework Tech
6 West River Street #225
Milford, CT 06460

Note that this notice informs readers that all rights are reserved and prohibits the reproduction or transmission of any part of the book without written permission from the author. It also allows for the inclusion of brief quotations in a review, in accordance with fair use laws.

Join The Framework Tech Community

In addition to our weekly tech talk show, each week we produce videos, tutorials, and articles for people who want to learn new digital skills.

Join us free at **FrameworkTV.com**.

Table of Contents

How to Use This Book

This book was designed to provide a quick and easy reference to the HTML5 language. The book provides a description of all HTML5 tags defining each tag, explaining its usage and listing example code.

A list of attributes that modify each tag is included as well. Please note that all tags are modified by the global HTML attributes, described at the end of this book.

I hope you will keep this guide on your desk and refer to it often as you build correct and maintainable HTML code.

Quick Intro: Elements, Tags, Attributes and Values

HTML (Hypertext Markup Language) is the standard markup language for creating web pages. It consists of various elements, tags, attributes, and values that define the structure and presentation of content on the web.

Elements

Elements are the building blocks of HTML documents. They represent different types of content and provide structure to the web page. Each element is enclosed within opening and closing tags. Here are a few examples:

- `<p>`: Represents a paragraph of text.
- `<h1>` to `<h6>`: Represents heading levels from 1 to 6.
- `<img>`: Represents an image.
- `<a>`: Represents a hyperlink.

Example code:

```
<p>This is a paragraph of text.</p>
<h1>This is a heading level 1</h1>
<img src="image.jpg" alt="Description of the im
age">
<a href="https://www.example.com">Visit Example
.com</a>
```

Tags

Tags are used to define elements in HTML. They consist of an opening tag, content, and a closing tag. The opening tag begins with < and ends with >, while the closing tag begins with </ and ends with >. Here's an example:

```
<p>This is a paragraph of text.</p>
```

In the above example, <p> is the opening tag, This is a paragraph of text. is the content, and </p> is the closing tag.

Attributes

Attributes provide additional information about HTML elements. They are specified within the opening tag and consist of a name-value pair. Here's an example:

```
<a href="https://www.example.com">Visit Example
.com</a>
```

In the above example, href is the attribute name, and "https://www.example.com" is the attribute value. ## Values Attribute values define the specific value assigned to an attribute. They can be assigned using quotes (") or single quotes ('). Here's an example:

```
<a href="https://www.example.com">Visit Example
.com</a>
```

In the above example, `"https://www.example.com"` is the attribute value.

This HTML dictionary provides a comprehensive reference of HTML elements, tags, attributes, and values that you can use to build web pages. Each entry includes a definition, usage, and code examples to help you understand and implement HTML effectively.

Feel free to explore the dictionary and refer to it whenever you need guidance on specific HTML elements and their usage.

The HTML5 Standard

The HTML5 Dictionary goes beyond the basics and delves into the powerful features and enhancements introduced by the HTML5 standard.

HTML5 revolutionized web development by introducing new elements, attributes, and APIs that enable developers to create more interactive and dynamic websites. This handbook provides an up-to-date exploration of HTML5, equipping you with the knowledge to leverage its latest capabilities and take advantage of its improved multimedia support, form validation, offline browsing, and much more.

Semantic Code

One of the key focuses of this book is semantic coding. Semantic HTML is a fundamental principle of modern web development, emphasizing the use of appropriate elements to convey the structure and meaning of the content.

By adopting semantic coding practices, you ensure that your websites are not only well-organized but also accessible and search engine-friendly. With clear examples and best practices, this handbook guides you in using semantic HTML5 elements to their fullest potential, enhancing the structure and clarity of your web pages while improving the overall user experience.

`<a>`

Definition: The `<a>` HTML element (or anchor element) creates a hyperlink to other web pages, files, locations within the same page, email addresses, or any other URL.

Usage: It's used when you want to create a link that navigates to another page, a different section of the same page, or opens a new email message.

Code Example:

```
<a href="https://www.example.com">Visit Example
.com</a>
```

Attributes

`href`: Specifies the URL of the page the link goes to

`target`: Specifies where to open the linked document. Possible values: `_blank` (opens in new tab), `_self` (opens in same frame as it was clicked), `_parent` (opens in parent frame), `_top` (opens in full body of the window).

`download`: Specifies that the target will be downloaded when a user clicks on the hyperlink.

`rel`: Specifies the relationship between the current document and the linked document.

`hreflang`: Specifies the language of the linked resource.

`type`: Specifies the MIME type of the linked resource.

`ping`: Contains space-separated list of URLs to which, when the hyperlink is followed, post requests with the body `PING` will be sent by the browser (in the background).

Browser Compatibility: The `<a>` element is widely supported across all major browsers.

Accessibility Considerations: Ensure the link has a focus state for those navigating via keyboard. Use clear language for the link text, so users know where the link will take them.

`<abbr>`

Definition: The `<abbr>` HTML element represents an abbreviation or acronym; the optional `title` attribute can provide an expansion or description for the abbreviation.

Usage: It's used when you want to use an abbreviation or an acronym, and also provide a full description for it.

Code Example:

```
<abbr title="Hyper Text Markup Language">HTML</abbr>
```

Attributes
`title`: Contains a full description of the abbreviation.

<address>

Definition: The <address> HTML element indicates that the enclosed HTML provides contact information for a person or people, or for an organization.

Usage: It's used when you want to provide contact information.

Code Example:

```
<address>
  Written by <a href="mailto:webmaster@example.
com">Jon Doe</a>.<br>
  Visit us at:<br>
  Example.com<br>
  Box 564, Disneyland<br>
  USA
</address>
```

Attributes
This tag doesn't have any specific attributes, it only uses global HTML attributes.

<area>

Definition: The <area> HTML element defines a hot-spot region on an image, and optionally associates it with a hypertext link. This element is used only within a <map> element.

Usage: It's used when you want to create an image map, which is an image with clickable areas.

Code Example:

```
<img src="planets.gif" width="145" height="126"
alt="Planets" usemap="#planetmap">

<map name="planetmap">
  <area shape="rect" coords="0,0,82,126" href="
sun.htm" alt="Sun">
  <area shape="circle" coords="90,58,3" href="m
ercur.htm" alt="Mercury">
  <area shape="circle" coords="124,58,8" href="
venus.htm" alt="Venus">
</map>
```

Attributes

shape: Specifies the shape of the area. Possible values: default, rect, circle, poly.

coords: A set of values specifying the coordinates of the hot-spot region.

href: Specifies the URL of the page the link goes to.

alt: Specifies an alternative text for the area. Required if the href attribute is present.

target: Specifies where to open the linked document.

<article>

Definition: The <article> HTML element represents a self-contained composition in a document, page, application, or site, which is intended to be independently distributable or reusable.

Usage: It's used to mark up a self-contained piece of content that could be distributed to other websites or platforms.

Code Example:

```
<article>
  <h2>My First Article</h2>
  <p>This is the content of my first article.</
p>
</article>
```

Attributes
This tag doesn't have any specific attributes, it only uses global HTML attributes.

`<aside>`

Definition: The `<aside>` HTML element represents a portion of a document whose content is only indirectly related to the document's main content.

Usage: It's used to mark up content that is separate from the main content of a webpage, such as sidebars, pull quotes, or advertising.

Code Example:

```
<article>
  <h2>My Article</h2>
  <p>This is the content of my article.</p>
  <aside>This is a sidebar related to the artic
le.</aside>
</article>
```

Attributes
This tag doesn't have any specific attributes, it only uses global HTML attributes.

`<audio>`

Definition: The `<audio>` HTML element is used to embed sound content in documents. It may contain one or more audio sources, represented using the `src` attribute or the `source` element.

Usage: It's used when you want to embed sound or music in your web pages.

Code Example:

```
<audio controls>
  <source src="myAudio.mp3" type="audio/mpeg">
  Your browser does not support the audio eleme
nt.
</audio>
```

Attributes

src: Specifies the URL of the audio file.

controls: Adds audio controls, like play, pause, and volume.

autoplay: Specifies that the audio will start playing as soon as it is ready.

loop: Specifies that the audio will start over again, every time it is finished.

muted: Specifies that the audio output should be muted.

preload: Specifies if and how the author thinks the audio should be loaded when the page loads. Possible values: auto, metadata, none.

crossorigin: This attribute controls how the element handles crossorigin requests, governing how the element handles CORS and credentials.

buffered: This read-only attribute tells the time range of already buffered media.

currentTime: This attribute gets and sets the current playback time in seconds.

duration: A read-only attribute, it indicates the total duration of the media in seconds.

played: A read-only attribute, it represents the ranges of the media source that the browser has played, given as a normalized TimeRanges object.

Browser Compatibility: The <audio> element is widely supported across all major browsers.

Accessibility Considerations: When using the <audio> element, always provide controls for the audio. Make sure to include a text transcript or description for audio content to make it accessible to all users.

`<b>`

Definition: The `<b>` HTML element is used to draw the reader's attention to the element's contents, which are not otherwise granted special importance.

Usage: It's used to style a part of the text without conveying any special importance or relevance.

Code Example:

```
<p>The <b>b</b> element is used to draw attention to enclosed text without implying any added importance or emphasis.</p>
```

Attributes
This tag doesn't have any specific attributes, it only uses global HTML attributes.

Browser Compatibility: The `<b>` element is widely supported across all major browsers.

Accessibility Considerations: This tag doesn't convey any special semantic meaning, so it doesn't affect the accessibility tree.

<base>

Definition: The `<base>` HTML element specifies the base URL to use for all relative URLs contained within a document.

Usage: It's used when you want to specify a base URL for all the links in a page.

Code Example:

```
<head>
  <base href="https://www.example.com/" target="_blank">
</head>
```

Attributes
`href`: Specifies the base URL for all relative URLs in the page.

`target`: Specifies the default target for all hyperlinks and forms in the page.

Browser Compatibility: The `<base>` element is widely supported across all major browsers.

Accessibility Considerations: This tag doesn't have any direct impact on accessibility.

<bdi>

Definition: The `<bdi>` (Bi-Directional Isolation) HTML element isolates a span of text that might be formatted in a different direction from other text outside it.

Usage: It's used when dealing with text that might have a different directionality from its surrounding text.

Code Example:

```
<p>User comments: <bdi>טקסט בעברית</bdi></p>
```

Attributes
dir: Specifies the text direction. Possible values are ltr (left-to-right) and rtl (right-to-left).

Browser Compatibility: The <bdi> element is supported in most modern browsers, but it is not supported in Internet Explorer.

Accessibility Considerations: Use this tag to improve the reading experience for users who rely on assistive technology to read content in languages written from right-to-left.

<bdo>

Definition: The <bdo> HTML element overrides the current text directionality.

Usage: It's used when you want to override the text direction.

Code Example:

```
<p><bdo dir="rtl">This text will go right to le
ft.</bdo></p>
```

Attributes
dir: Specifies the text direction. Possible values are ltr (left-to-right) and rtl (right-to-left).

Browser Compatibility: The <bdo> element is widely supported across all major browsers.

Accessibility Considerations: Use this tag to improve the reading experience for users who read content in languages written from right-to-left.

`<blockquote>`

Definition: The `<blockquote>` HTML element indicates that the enclosed text is an extended quotation.

Usage: It's used when you want to quote a chunk of content from a different source.

Code Example:

```
<blockquote cite="https://www.example.com/">
  <p>This is a quotation taken from the Example
.com website
  <p>This is a quotation taken from the Example
.com website.</p>
</blockquote>
```

Attributes

`cite`: Specifies the URL of the quote's source.

Browser Compatibility: The `<blockquote>` element is widely supported across all major browsers.

Accessibility Considerations: Use the `cite` attribute to reference the source of the quote, providing more context for assistive technologies.

`<body>`

Definition: The `<body>` HTML element represents the content of an HTML document.

Usage: All the content inside `<body>` appears on the web page. It contains all the contents of an HTML document, such as text, hyperlinks, images, tables, lists, etc.

Code Example:

```
<body>
  <h1>This is a heading</h1>
  <p>This is a paragraph.</p>
  <p>This is another paragraph.</p>
</body>
```

Attributes
This tag doesn't have any specific attributes, it only uses global HTML attributes.

Browser Compatibility: The <body> element is widely supported across all major browsers.

Accessibility Considerations: The <body> element doesn't directly affect accessibility, but all content within it should follow best practices for web accessibility.

Definition: The
 HTML element produces a line break in text (carriage-return).

Usage: It's used when you want to create a line break.

Code Example:

```
<p>This is a paragraph with a line break.<br> The text continues on the next line.</p>
```

Attributes
This tag doesn't have any specific attributes, it only uses global HTML attributes.

Browser Compatibility: The <br> element is widely supported across all major browsers.

Accessibility Considerations: Use line breaks sparingly as they can disrupt the reading flow for screen reader users.

`<button>`

Definition: The `<button>` HTML element represents a clickable button.

Usage: It's used when you want to create a button.

Code Example:

```
<button type="button" onclick="alert('Hello Wor
ld!')">Click Me!</button>
```

Attributes
`disabled`: Indicates that the button should be disabled and is not selectable.

`form`: Associates the button with a form.

`type`: Specifies the type of button. Possible values: `submit`, `reset`, `button`.

`value`: Defines a default value which will be sent when the form is submitted.

Browser Compatibility: The `<button>` element is widely supported across all major browsers.

Accessibility Considerations: Always provide an accessible name for the button either using inner text or the `aria-label` attribute for those who use screen readers. Avoid using `<button>` elements for page sections that are not traditionally expected to be interactive.

`<canvas>`

Definition: The `<canvas>` HTML element is used to draw graphics on a web page.

Usage: It's used when you want to render graphics, game graphics, art, or other visual images on the fly.

Code Example:

```
<canvas id="myCanvas" width="200" height="100"
style="border:1px solid #000000;"></canvas>
```

Attributes width: Specifies the width of the canvas. - height: Specifies the height of the canvas.

Browser Compatibility: The `<canvas>` element is widely supported across all major browsers.

Accessibility Considerations: For accessibility, always provide a fallback for the `<canvas>` element for browsers that don't support it. Additionally, a text equivalent for the canvas content should be provided inside the `<canvas>` tag for screen reader users.

<caption>

Definition: The <caption> HTML element specifies the caption (or title) of a table.

Usage: It's used when you want to add a title to your table.

Code Example:

```
<table>
  <caption>Monthly savings</caption>
  <tr>
    <th>Month</th>
    <th>Savings</th>
  </tr>
  <tr>
    <td>January</td>
    <td>$100</td>
  </tr>
</table>
```

Attributes tag doesn't have any specific attributes, it only uses global HTML attributes.

Browser Compatibility: The <caption> element is widely supported across all major browsers.

Accessibility Considerations: The <caption> element improves accessibility by providing a way to associate a text description with a table that users can read or listen to.

<cite>

Definition: The <cite> HTML element is used to describe a reference to a cited creative work.

Usage: It's used when you want to reference a book, a song, a movie, a TV show, a painting, a sculpture, or any other work.

Code Example:

```
<p><cite>The Scream</cite> by Edward Munch. Painted in 1893.</p>
```

Attributes
This tag doesn't have any specific attributes, it only uses global HTML attributes.

Browser Compatibility: The `<cite>` element is widely supported across all major browsers.

Accessibility Considerations: This tag doesn't directly affect accessibility, but it's good practice to provide a reference to any cited creative work.

`<code>`

Definition: The `<code>` HTML element is used to display a fragment of computer code.

Usage: It's used when you want to display code snippets in your web page.

Code Example:

```
<p>The following HTML markup: <code>&lt;p&gt;This is a paragraph.&lt;/p&gt;</code> creates a paragraph.</p>
```

Attributes
This tag doesn't have any specific attributes, it only uses global HTML attributes.

Browser Compatibility: The <code> element is widely supported across all major browsers.

Accessibility Considerations: This tag doesn't directly affect accessibility. However, it might be helpful to screen reader users to indicate that the text is a short inline snippet of code.

<col>

Definition: The <col> HTML element specifies column properties for each column within a <colgroup> element.

Usage: It's used when you want to specify styles for one or more columns in a table.

Code Example:

```
<table>
  <colgroup>
    <col span="2" style="background-color:red">
    <col style="background-color:yellow">
  </colgroup>
  <tr>
    <th>ISBN</th>
    <th>Title</th>
    <th>Price</th>
  </tr>
  <tr>
    <td>3476896</td>
    <td>My Book</td>
    <td>$90</td>
  </tr>
</table>
```

Attributes

span: Specifies how many columns in a column group a <col> element should span.

width: Specifies the width of the columns.

Browser Compatibility: The <col> element is widely supported across all major browsers.

Accessibility Considerations: This tag doesn't directly affect accessibility. However, using it to manage the layout of tables can make the tables easier to understand for screen reader users.

<colgroup>

Definition: The <colgroup> HTML element is used to group one or more <col> elements in a table.

Usage: It's used when you want to apply styles to entire columns, instead of repeating the styles for each cell, for each row.

Code Example:

```
<table>
  <colgroup>
    <col span="2" style="background-color:red">
    <col style="background-color:yellow">
  </colgroup>
  <tr>
    <th>ISBN</th>
    <th>Title</th>
    <th>Price</th>
  </tr>
  <tr>
    <td>3476896</td>
    <td>My Book</td>
    <td>$90</td>
```

```
  </tr>
</table>
```

Attributes

span: Specifies how many columns to span.

Browser Compatibility: The `<colgroup>` element is widely supported across all major browsers.

Accessibility Considerations: This tag doesn't directly affect accessibility. However, using it to manage the layout of tables can make the tables easier to understand for screen reader users.

<datalist>

Definition: The <datalist> HTML element contains a set of <option> elements that represent the permissible or recommended options available to choose from within other controls.

Usage: It's used with an <input> element where the list attribute of the <input> element refers to the id of the <datalist> element.

Code Example:

```
<input list="browsers" name="myBrowser" id="myB
rowser">
<datalist id="browsers">
  <option value="Chrome">
  <option value="Firefox">
  <option value="Safari">
  <option value="Opera">
  <option value="Internet Explorer">
</datalist>
```

Attributes

This tag doesn't have any specific attributes, it only uses global HTML attributes.

Browser Compatibility: The `<datalist>` element is widely supported across all major browsers.

Accessibility Considerations: Be aware that screen readers do not always interact well with this element. Ensure to provide appropriate labels and instructions to aid accessibility.

`<dd>`

Definition: The `<dd>` HTML element provides the description, definition, or value for the preceding term (`<dt>`) in a description list (`<dl>`).

Usage: It's used within a `<dl>` (description list) element to provide descriptions, definitions, or values that correspond to a specific term in a list.

Code Example:

```
<dl>
  <dt>Coffee</dt>
  <dd>Black hot drink</dd>
  <dt>Milk</dt>
  <dd>White cold drink</dd>
</dl>
```

Attributes

This tag doesn't have any specific attributes, it only uses global HTML attributes.

Browser Compatibility: The `<dd>` element is widely supported across all major browsers.

Accessibility Considerations: Ensure the context and relationship between the `<dt>` and `<dd>` elements is clear to assist those using screen readers.

`<del>`

Definition: The `<del>` HTML element represents a range of text that has been deleted from a document.

Usage: It's used to markup deletions in your document. This can be useful when you want to show the changes that have been made to a document.

Code Example:

```
<p>My favorite color is <del>blue</del> red.</p>
```

Attributes
`cite`: Specifies a URL to a document that explains why the text was deleted. - `datetime`: Specifies the date and time when the text was deleted.

Browser Compatibility: The `<del>` element is widely supported across all major browsers.

Accessibility Considerations: It's important to make sure that the content remains understandable, even if the information inside `<del>` is removed. The use of `cite` and `datetime` can provide additional context.

`<details>`

Definition: The `<details>` HTML element creates a disclosure widget in which information is visible only when the widget is toggled into an "open" state.

Usage: It's used when you want to hide some content that is not directly necessary, but that users can expand to see if they wish.

Code Example:

```
<details>
  <summary>Epcot Center</summary>
  <p>Epcot is a theme park at Walt Disney World
Resort featuring exciting attractions, internat
ional pavilions, award-winning fireworks and se
asonal special events.</p>
</details>
```

Attributes
open: Specifies that the details should be visible (open) to the user. If not specified, the details are not visible.

Browser Compatibility: The `<details>` element is widely supported across all major browsers, except Internet Explorer.

Accessibility Considerations: Always use the `<summary>` element as a child of the `<details>` element to provide a description. Some older screen readers do not support this element, consider providing additional mechanisms to view the content.

`<dfn>`

Definition: The `<dfn>` HTML element represents the defining instance of a term in HTML.

Usage: It's used when you want to introduce a term for the first time in a document or a section of a document, like a scientific paper or a tutorial.

Code Example:

```
<p>The <dfn id="def-internet">Internet</dfn> is
the global system of interconnected networks th
at use the Internet protocol suite (TCP/IP).</p
>
```

Attributes

This tag doesn't have any specific attributes, it only uses global HTML attributes.

Browser Compatibility: The `<dfn>` element is widely supported across all major browsers.

Accessibility Considerations: It's a good idea to always pair the `<dfn>` element with a `<a>` element using the `href` attribute to link back to the definition for easy navigation.

`<dialog>`

Definition: The `<dialog>` HTML element represents a dialog box or other interactive component, such as a dismissible alert, inspector, or subwindow.

Usage: It's used when you want to create pop-up dialogs or modal windows on a webpage.

Code Example:

```
<dialog open>
   This is an open dialog window.
</dialog>
```

Attributes

open: Specifies that the dialog should be open and visible. If not specified, the dialog is not open.

returnvalue: Holds the return value when the dialog is closed.

Browser Compatibility: The `<dialog>` element is not supported in Internet Explorer and has limited support in some other browsers.

Accessibility Considerations: Ensure to manage focus properly when using dialog, and provide a clear way to close the dialog. Use ARIA roles and properties when necessary for better screen reader support.

`<em>`

Definition: The `<em>` HTML element marks text that has stress emphasis.

Usage: It's used when you want to emphasize a certain word or phrase within a block of text. This is typically displayed in italic type by the browser.

Code Example:

```
<p>I <em>really</em> need to go to the
supermarket.</p>
```

Attributes
This tag doesn't have any specific attributes, it only uses global HTML attributes.

Browser Compatibility: The `<em>` element is widely supported across all major browsers.

Accessibility Considerations: Use the `<em>` element when you want to emphasize something. Do not use it for styling purposes, use CSS for that.

<embed>

Definition: The <embed> HTML element embeds external content at the specified point in the document.

Usage: It's used when you want to include external content, such as a video, into your web page.

Code Example:

```
<embed type="video/webm" src="myVideo.webm" width="400" height="300">
```

Attributes

src: Specifies the URL of the resource being embedded.

type: Specifies the MIME type of the resource being embedded.

width and height: Specifies the dimensions of the embedded content.

Browser Compatibility: The <embed> element is widely supported across all major browsers.

Accessibility Considerations: Keep in mind that not all types of embedded content are accessible to all users. Provide alternative content or descriptions when necessary.

`<fieldset>`

Definition: The `<fieldset>` HTML element is used to group several controls as well as labels (`<label>`) within a web form.

Usage: It's used when you want to group related form controls and labels together, which can make it easier for users to interact with your form.

Code Example:

```
<form>
  <fieldset>
    <legend>Personalia:</legend>
    <label for="fname">First name:</label><br>
    <input type="text" id="fname" name="fname">
<br>
    <label for="lname">Last name:</label><br>
    <input type="text" id="lname" name="lname">
  </fieldset>
</form>
```

Attributes

`disabled`: Specifies that all form controls within the fieldset should be disabled.

`form`: Specifies one or more forms the fieldset belongs to.

`name`: Specifies the name of the fieldset.

Browser Compatibility: The `<fieldset>` element is widely supported across all major browsers.

Accessibility Considerations: Use the `<legend>` element to provide a description of the group. Ensure that all form controls are properly labeled.

`<figcaption>`

Definition: The `<figcaption>` HTML element represents a caption or a legend associated with a figure or an illustration described by the rest of the data of the `<figure>` element the caption is included in.

Usage: It's used within a `<figure>` element to provide a caption for the content of the figure.

Code Example:

```
<figure>
  <img src="myImage.jpg" alt="An awesome pictur
e">
  <figcaption>This is an awesome picture</figca
ption>
</figure>
```

Attributes

This tag doesn't have any specific attributes, it only uses global HTML attributes.

Browser Compatibility: The `<figcaption>` element is widely supported across all major browsers.

Accessibility Considerations: Ensure that the caption effectively describes the content of the figure. When the figure element is not used with a figcaption, the figure element should be marked with the `role="presentation"` or `role="none"` attribute.

`<figure>`

Definition: The `<figure>` HTML element represents self-contained content, potentially with an optional caption, which is specified using the (`<figcaption>`) element.

Usage: It's used when you want to include content such as illustrations, diagrams, photos, code listings, etc., that is referenced from the main content, but can be moved away from that primary content without affecting the document's meaning.

Code Example:

```
<figure>
  <img src="myImage.jpg" alt="An awesome pictur
e">
  <figcaption>This is an awesome picture</figca
ption>
</figure>
```

Attributes
This tag doesn't have any specific attributes, it only uses global HTML attributes.

Browser Compatibility: The `<figure>` element is widely supported across all major browsers.

Accessibility Considerations: Always provide a useful caption using `<figcaption>` for each `<figure>` and provide alternative text for the images. For screen reader users, consider using ARIA roles and properties to enhance the semantics of the figure and figcaption elements.

`<footer>`

Definition: The `<footer>` HTML element represents a footer for its nearest sectioning content or sectioning root element. It typically contains information about the author of the section, copyright data, or links to related documents.

Usage: It's used when you want to specify a footer for a document or a section. This can contain information about the author, copyright information, etc.

Code Example:

```
<footer>
  <p>Posted by: John Doe</p>
  <p>Contact information: <a href="mailto:someo
ne@example.com">someone@example.com</a>.</p>
</footer>
```

Attributes
This tag doesn't have any specific attributes, it only uses global HTML attributes.

Browser Compatibility: The `<footer>` element is widely supported across all major browsers.

Accessibility Considerations: Use clear and descriptive information in the footer. Avoid using important navigation links or performing key tasks as footers can sometimes be skipped by screen reader users.

`<h1>`, `<h2>`, `<h3>`, `<h4>`, `<h5>`, `<h6>`

Definition: The `<h1>`, `<h2>`, `<h3>`, `<h4>`, `<h5>`, and `<h6>` HTML elements represent six levels of section headings, `<h1>` is the highest and `<h6>` is the lowest.

Usage: They're used to mark the headings of sections, with `<h1>` being the main heading, and `<h2>` to `<h6>` being subheadings.

Code Example:

```
<h1>This is a main heading</h1>
<h2>This is a subheading</h2>
<h3>This is a sub-subheading</h3>
<!-- And so on -->
```

Attributes
These tags don't have any specific attributes, they only use global HTML attributes.

Browser Compatibility: The heading elements are widely supported across all major browsers.

Accessibility Considerations: Screen readers use these to enable keyboard shortcut navigation, so ensure to use them in hierarchical order.

‹head›

Definition: The ‹head› HTML element contains machine-readable information (metadata) about the document, like its title, scripts, and style sheets.

Usage: It's used to contain metadata for the web page, such as the title and links to scripts and stylesheets.

Code Example:

```
<head>
  <title>Page Title</title>
  <link rel="stylesheet" href="styles.css">
  <script src="script.js"></script>
</head>
```

Attributes
This tag doesn't have any specific attributes, it only uses global HTML attributes.

Browser Compatibility: The ‹head› element is widely supported across all major browsers.

Accessibility Considerations: Most of the elements inside ‹head› do not affect the display, but the ‹title› is important for accessibility and for SEO.

‹header›

Definition: The ‹header› HTML element represents introductory content, typically a group of introductory or navigational aids. It may contain some heading elements but also other elements like a logo, wrapped section's header, a search form, and so on.

Usage: It's used when you want to specify a header for a document or a section.

Code Example:

```
<header>
  <h1>Welcome to My Website</h1>
  <p>This is the site header, containing a titl
e and a subtitle</p>
</header>
```

Attributes
This tag doesn't have any specific attributes, it only uses global HTML attributes.

Browser Compatibility: The `<header>` element is widely supported across all major browsers.

Accessibility Considerations: Structure your header in a meaningful way, use headings to outline the content.

`<hr>`

Definition: The `<hr>` HTML element represents a thematic break between paragraph-level elements: for example, a change of scene in a story, or a shift of topic within a section.

Usage: It's used when you want to insert a thematic break between the elements.

Code Example:

```
<p>This is the end of the first topic.</p>
<hr>
<p>Now we start a new topic.</p>
```

Attributes

This tag doesn't have any specific attributes, it only uses global HTML attributes.

Browser Compatibility: The <hr> element is widely supported across all major browsers.

Accessibility Considerations: The <hr> element is typically displayed as a horizontal rule. However, it should be used to represent a semantic shift in content rather than for its visual presentation. For cosmetic horizontal rules, consider using CSS borders instead.

<html>

Definition: The <html> HTML element represents the root (top-level element) of an HTML document, so it is also referred to as the root element. All other elements must be descendants of this element.

Usage: It's used once in an HTML document to encapsulate the entire page content.

Code Example:

```
<!DOCTYPE html>
<html>
<head>
    <!-- head content goes here -->
</head>
<body>
    <!-- body content goes here -->
</body>
</html>
```

Attributes

manifest: Specifies the address of the document's cache

manifest. Deprecated as of HTML5. It's better to use service workers for offline apps.

xmlns: For XML, not used in HTML. This is the XML namespace.

lang: Declares the language of the page content, which aids in localization.

Browser Compatibility: The <html> element is universally supported across all major browsers.

Accessibility Considerations: The lang attribute on the <html> element is important for accessibility, as it helps screen readers determine the language for pronunciation.

`<i>`

Definition: The `<i>` HTML element represents a range of text that is set off from the normal text for some reason, such as idiomatic text, technical terms, taxonomical designations, among others.

Usage: It's used when you want to italicize text for reasons other than emphasis.

Code Example:

```
<p>The word <i>crepuscular</i> means "active du
ring twilight."</p>
```

Attributes
This tag doesn't have any specific attributes, it only uses global HTML attributes.

Browser Compatibility: The `<i>` element is widely supported across all major browsers.

Accessibility Considerations: Because some screen readers do not announce the presence of italicized text, use CSS to change the style of the text rather than the `<i>` tag if italics is the only change.

`<iframe>`

Definition: The `<iframe>` HTML element represents a nested browsing context, effectively embedding another HTML page into the current page.

Usage: It's used when you want to embed another document within the current HTML document.

Code Example:

```
<iframe src="https://www.example.com" title="Example Website"></iframe>
```

Attributes
`src`: Specifies the URL of the page to embed.

`height` and `width`: Set the dimensions of the iframe. - `name`: Specifies the name of the iframe.

`sandbox`: Enables an extra set of restrictions for the content in the iframe.

`srcdoc`: Specifies the HTML content of the page to show in the iframe.

`title`: Provides a title for the iframe which is used by screen readers.

Browser Compatibility: The `<iframe>` element is widely supported across all major browsers.

Accessibility Considerations: Always provide a `title` attribute (accessible name) to an iframe for screen reader users.

`<img>`

Definition: The `<img>` HTML element embeds an image into the document.

Usage: It's used when you want to insert an image in the HTML document.

Code Example:

```html
<img src="myImage.jpg" alt="A description of th
e image" width="500" height="600">
```

Attributes
`src`: Specifies the URL of the image.

`alt`: Provides alternative information for an image if a user for some reason cannot view it.

`height` and `width`: Specify the dimensions of the image.

Browser Compatibility: The `<img>` element is widely supported across all major browsers.

Accessibility Considerations: Always provide a meaningful `alt` attribute for those who cannot see the image. If the image is decorative and doesn't convey meaningful content, use `alt=""`.

`<input>`

Definition: The `<input>` HTML element is used to create interactive controls for web-based forms in order to accept data from the user.

Usage: It's used to create different types of input fields, like text fields, checkboxes, radio buttons, submit buttons, and more.

Code Example:

```
<form action="/submit_form">
  First name: <input type="text" name="fname"><
br>
  Last name: <input type="text" name="lname"><b
r>
  <input type="submit" value="Submit">
</form>
```

Attributes

type: Specifies the type of input element to display.

name: Specifies the name for the input element.

value: Specifies the initial value for the input element.

placeholder: Specifies a short hint that describes the expected value of an input field.

required: Specifies that an input field must be filled out before submitting the form.

readonly: Specifies that an input field is read-only (cannot be changed).

disabled: Specifies that an input field should be disabled.

autocomplete: Specifies whether the browser should enable autocomplete for the input field.

Browser Compatibility: The <input> element is widely supported across all major browsers. However, different type values can have varying levels of support.

Accessibility Considerations: Always pair an input with a <label> element. Screen readers will read the label when the user is focused on the form input.

`<ins>`

Definition: The `<ins>` HTML element represents a range of text that has been added to a document.

Usage: It's used when you want to indicate that certain text has been inserted into a document.

Code Example:

```
<p>My favorite color is <ins>blue</ins>.</p>
```

Attributes
`cite`: Contains a URL that explains the changes. - `datetime`: Specifies the date and time when the text was inserted.

Browser Compatibility: The `<ins>` element is widely supported across all major browsers.

Accessibility Considerations: There are no specific accessibility considerations for the `<ins>` tag.

`<kbd>`

Definition: The `<kbd>` HTML element represents user input and produces an inline element displayed in the browser's default monospace font.

Usage: It's used when you want to denote user keyboard input, voice commands, or any other type of user inputs.

Code Example:

```
<p>To save the document, press <kbd>Ctrl+S</kbd>.</p>
```

Attributes
This tag doesn't have any specific attributes, it only uses global HTML attributes.

Browser Compatibility: The `<kbd>` element is widely supported across all major browsers.

Accessibility Considerations: There are no specific accessibility considerations for the `<kbd>` tag.

`<label>`

Definition: The `<label>` HTML element represents a caption for an item in a user interface.

Usage: It's used to associate a text label with a form control, like an `<input>`, `<select>`, `<textarea>`, etc. This is especially helpful for accessibility as screen readers read the associated label when the user is focused on the form element.

Code Example:

```html
<label for="fname">First name:</label>
<input type="text" id="fname" name="fname">
```

Attributes

`for`: Specifies which form element a label is bound to.

Browser Compatibility: The `<label>` element is widely supported across all major browsers.

Accessibility Considerations: Always use a `<label>` for form inputs. Screen readers will read the label when the user is focused on the form input.

<legend>

Definition: The <legend> HTML element represents a caption for the content of its parent <fieldset>.

Usage: It's used to provide a title or description for a group of related form elements that are grouped together into a <fieldset>.

Code Example:

```
<fieldset>
  <legend>Personalia:</legend>
  Name: <input type="text"><br>
  Email: <input type="text"><br>
  Date of birth: <input type="text">
</fieldset>
```

Attributes
This tag doesn't have any specific attributes, it only uses global HTML attributes.

Browser Compatibility: The <legend> element is widely supported across all major browsers.

Accessibility Considerations: Always use a <legend> to describe the group of related inputs in a <fieldset>. Screen readers will read the legend when the user is focused on an input within the fieldset.

<li>

Definition: The <li> HTML element is used to represent an item in a list.

Usage: It's used within parent elements like <ul> (unordered list), <ol> (ordered list), and <menu> (menu list).

Code Example:

```
<ul>
   <li>Coffee</li>
   <li>Tea</li>
   <li>Milk</li>
</ul>
```

Attributes

value: This attribute is used in ordered lists, that is, within <ol> elements, where it serves to define the value of the list item. The value attribute must be a number and it will define the number that the list item will start from.

Browser Compatibility: The <li> element is widely supported across all major browsers.

Accessibility Considerations: Use <li> within a parent list element (<ul>, <ol>, or <menu>) for proper semantics and accessibility.

`<main>`

Definition: The `<main>` HTML element represents the dominant content of the `<body>` of a document. The main content area consists of content that is directly related to or expands upon the central topic of a document, or the central functionality of an application.

Usage: It's used to wrap the main content of a document excluding items that are repeated across a set of documents such as site navigation links, header or footer.

Code Example:

```
<main>
  <h1>Welcome to my homepage</h1>
  <p>This is the main content of my website.</p>
</main>
```

Attributes

This tag doesn't have any specific attributes, it only uses global HTML attributes.

Browser Compatibility: The `<main>` element is widely supported across all major browsers.

Accessibility Considerations: There should be only one `<main>` tag per page and it should be unique to the document, excluding content that is repeated across a set of documents such as navigation links, header, or footer.

`<map>`

Definition: The `<map>` HTML element is used with `<area>` elements to define an image map (a clickable link area).

Usage: It's used to create an image map. The `<map>` tag is not used alone, it must be used with the following tags: `<area>` and `<img>`.

Code Example:

```
<img src="planets.gif" width="145" height="126"
alt="Planets" usemap="#planetmap">

<map name="planetmap">
  <area shape="rect" coords="0,0,82,126" href="
sun.htm" alt="Sun">
  <area shape="circle" coords="90,58,3" href="m
ercur.htm" alt="Mercury">
  <area shape="circle" coords="124,58,8" href="
venus.htm" alt="Venus">
</map>
```

Attributes

name: Specifies the name of the image map.

Browser Compatibility: The `<map>` element is widely supported across all major browsers.

Accessibility Considerations: Use alternative text for the <img> and <area> elements.

<mark>

Definition: The <mark> HTML element represents text that is marked or highlighted for reference or notation purposes, due to the marked passage's relevance or importance in the enclosing context.

Usage: It's used to highlight parts of a text.

Code Example:

```
<p>Do not forget to buy <mark>milk</mark> today.</p>
```

Attributes
This tag doesn't have any specific attributes, it only uses global HTML attributes.

Browser Compatibility: The <mark> element is widely supported across all major browsers.

Accessibility Considerations: There are no specific accessibility considerations for the <mark> tag.

<menu>

Definition: The <menu> HTML element represents a group of commands that a user can perform or activate.

Usage: It's used to create a menu of commands. As of HTML5, it's used to create a context menu, which pops up when a user right-clicks an element that has a contextmenu attribute.

Code Example:

```
<menu type="context" id="mymenu">
  <menuitem label="First item" onclick="alert('
You clicked the first item!');"></menuitem>
  <menuitem label="Second item" onclick="  aler
t('You clicked the second item!');"></menuitem>
</menu>
<p contextmenu="mymenu">Right-click this text t
o see the context menu!</p>
```

Attributes

type: Specifies the type of menu to be displayed. As of HTML5, the only valid value is context.

label: Specifies the visible title of a menu.

Browser Compatibility: The <menu> element is not supported in Internet Explorer. Its support varies across browsers and is deprecated in HTML5.

Accessibility Considerations: <menu> and <menuitem> are not widely used due to inconsistent support across browsers. It's recommended to use alternative ways to create menus, such as using <ul> and <li> elements with appropriate ARIA roles.

<meta>

Definition: The <meta> HTML element represents metadata that cannot be represented by other HTML meta-related elements, like <base>, <link>, <script>, <style> or <title>.

Usage: It's used within the <head> element to specify the character set, page description, keywords, author, and other metadata. The metadata can be used by browsers (how to display content or reload page), search engines (keywords), or other web services.

Code Example:

```
<head>
  <meta charset="UTF-8">
  <meta name="description" content="Free Web tu
torials">
  <meta name="keywords" content="HTML, CSS, Jav
aScript">
  <meta name="author" content="John Doe">
  <meta name="viewport" content="width=device-w
idth, initial-scale=1.0">
</head>
```

Attributes

charset: Specifies the character encoding for the HTML document.

content: Specifies the value associated with the http-equiv or name attribute.

http-equiv: Provides an HTTP header for the information in the content attribute.

name: Specifies a name for the metadata.

Browser Compatibility: The <meta> element is widely supported across all major browsers.

Accessibility Considerations: The use of the <meta> tag isn't directly related to web accessibility, but it does have an effect on overall web usability.

`<nav>`

Definition: The `<nav>` HTML element represents a section of a page whose purpose is to provide navigation links, either within the current document or to other documents. Common examples of navigation sections are menus, tables of contents, and indexes.

Usage: It's used to wrap major navigational blocks on the site.

Code Example:

```
<nav>
  <a href="#section1">Section 1</a> |
  <a href="#section2">Section 2</a> |
  <a href="#section3">Section 3</a>
</nav>
```

Attributes
This tag doesn't have any specific attributes, it only uses global HTML attributes.

Browser Compatibility: The `<nav>` element is widely supported across all major browsers.

Accessibility Considerations: Use a <nav> element only for sections that consist of major navigational blocks. Screen readers allow users to skip directly to the navigation, so it's a good practice not to include too many links in a <nav> element.

<noframes>

Definition: The <noframes> HTML element provides content to be presented in browsers that don't support (or have disabled support for) the <frame> element.

Usage: It's used to provide an alternative content for users that have frames disabled in their browser or are using a browser that doesn't support frames.

Code Example:

```
<frameset cols="200, *">
  <frame src="menu.html">
  <frame src="content.html">
  <noframes>
    <body>
      Your browser does not support frames.
    </body>
  </noframes>
</frameset>
```

Attributes

This tag doesn't have any specific attributes, it only uses global HTML attributes.

Browser Compatibility: The <noframes> element is not supported in HTML5. It's supported in HTML 4.01 (the last version before HTML5) and in XHTML 1.0, but it's obsolete. Use CSS instead to control layout.

Accessibility Considerations: Using `<frame>` and `<noframes>` elements is not recommended. Instead, use CSS to layout and control the visual presentation of your pages.

`<noscript>`

Definition: The `<noscript>` HTML element defines a section of HTML to be inserted if a script type on the page is unsupported or if scripting is currently turned off in the browser.

Usage: It's used to provide an alternative content for users that have JavaScript disabled in their browser.

Code Example:

```
<script>
  document.write("Hello World!")
</script>
<noscript>Your browser does not support JavaScript!</noscript>
```

Attributes

This tag doesn't have any specific attributes, it only uses global HTML attributes.

Browser Compatibility: The `<noscript>` element is widely supported across all major browsers.

Accessibility Considerations: Providing an alternative for users who have disabled scripting can make the page more accessible. But remember, some users may have JavaScript enabled but blocked for specific sites or pages, so always use feature detection and progressive enhancement when using JavaScript.

`<object>`

Definition: The `<object>` HTML element represents an external resource, which can be treated as an image, a nested browsing context, or a resource to be handled by a plugin.

Usage: It's used to embed objects such as images, audio, videos, Java applets, and Flash animations.

Code Example:

```html
<object data="horse.wav">
  <param name="autoplay" value="true">
</object>
```

Attributes

`data`: Specifies the URL of the resource.

`type`: Specifies the media type of the resource.

`width`, `height`: Specifies the width and height of the element.

`name`: Specifies the name of the object.

usemap: Specifies the name of a client-side image map to be used with the object.

Browser Compatibility: The <object> element is widely supported across all major browsers.

Accessibility Considerations: It's a good practice to include a text description of the object directly in the HTML content. This way, if the object doesn't load, the user will at least be able to read the description.

<ol>

Definition: The <ol> HTML element represents an ordered list of items — typically rendered as a numbered list.

Usage: It's used when the order of the list's items is important, such as a recipe's instructions.

Code Example:

```
<ol>
  <li>Mix flour and sugar.</li>
  <li>Add eggs.</li>
  <li>Stir and bake.</li>
</ol>
```

Attributes
reversed: A Boolean attribute that reverses the order of the list items.

start: Defines the first value in an ordered list. type: Defines the kind of marker to use in the list. Possible values: 1, A, a, I, i.

Browser Compatibility: The <ol> element is widely supported across all major browsers.

Accessibility Considerations: It's important to use
<ol> and <li> to mark up ordered lists, as they provide
semantics that are useful for screen readers.

<optgroup>

Definition: The <optgroup> HTML element creates a
grouping of options within a <select> element.

Usage: It's used to group related options in a dropdown list.

Code Example:

```html
<select>
  <optgroup label="Swedish Cars">
    <option value="volvo">Volvo</option>
    <option value="saab">Saab</option>
  </optgroup>
  <optgroup label="German Cars">
    <option value="mercedes">Mercedes</option>
    <option value="audi">Audi</option>
  </optgroup>
</select>
```

Attributes
label: Specifies a label for an option-group.

disabled: Specifies that the option-group should be
disabled.

Browser Compatibility: The <optgroup> element is
widely supported across all major browsers.

Accessibility Considerations: The use of <optgroup>
can make dropdown lists easier to understand for users
of screen readers.

`<option>`

Definition: The `<option>` HTML element is used to define an item contained in a `<select>`, an `<optgroup>`, or a `<datalist>` element. As such, `<option>` can represent menu items in popups and other lists of items in an HTML document.

Usage: It's used to define the items users can select from a dropdown list.

Code Example:

```
<select>
  <option value="volvo">Volvo</option>
  <option value="saab">Saab</option>
  <option value="mercedes">Mercedes</option>
  <option value="audi">Audi</option>
</select>
```

Attributes

`disabled`: If this Boolean attribute is set, this option is not checkable.

`label`: Defines a string that labels the option.

`selected`: If this attribute is set, this option is preselected when the page loads.

`value`: Defines a value which will be sent to the server if this option is selected.

Browser Compatibility: The `<option>` element is widely supported across all major browsers.

Accessibility Considerations: If the list of options is long, consider using the `<optgroup>` element to group related options.

`<p>`

Definition: The `<p>` HTML element represents a paragraph.

Usage: It's used to group a set of sentences in a paragraph.

Code Example:

```
<p>This is a simple paragraph.</p>
```

Attributes
This tag doesn't have any specific attributes; it only uses global HTML attributes.

Browser Compatibility: The `<p>` element is widely supported across all major browsers.

Accessibility Considerations: Although `<p>` tags do not typically need additional accessibility considerations, remember to use proper punctuation and formatting to help screen readers convey the text correctly.

`<param>`

Definition: The `<param>` HTML element defines parameters for an `<object>` element.

Usage: It's used to specify the runtime settings for an object loaded by the `<object>` element.

Code Example:

```
<object data="horse.wav">
  <param name="autoplay" value="true">
</object>
```

Attributes
name: Specifies the name of the parameter. - `value`: Specifies the value of the parameter.

Browser Compatibility: The `<param>` element is widely supported across all major browsers.

Accessibility Considerations: Parameters set with the `<param>` element should not have significant impact on accessibility. Remember to provide alternative content in case the object can't be displayed.

`<picture>`

Definition: The `<picture>` HTML element contains zero or more `<source>` elements and one `<img>` element to offer alternative versions of an image for different display/device scenarios.

Usage: It's used when you want to deliver optimized images for different display or device scenarios.

Code Example:

```
<picture>
  <source media="(min-width:650px)" srcset="img
_pink_flowers.jpg">
  <source media="(min-width:465px)" srcset="img
_white_flower.jpg">
  <img src="img_orange_flowers.jpg" alt="Flower
s">
</picture>
```

Attributes

The `<picture>` element does not have any specific attributes. It contains `source` elements which have `srcset` and `media` attributes, and an `img` element with `src` and `alt` attributes.

Browser Compatibility: The `<picture>` element is widely supported across all major browsers, but with some exceptions in older versions.

Accessibility Considerations: Always provide an `alt` attribute for the contained `img` element to describe the image to people who cannot see it.

`<pre>`

Definition: The `<pre>` HTML element represents preformatted text which is to be presented exactly as written in the HTML file.

Usage: It's used when you want to preserve both spaces and line breaks as typed, such as in a poem or a block of code.

Code Example:

```
<pre>
  function helloWorld() {
    console.log("Hello, world!");
```

```
   }
</pre>
```

Attributes
This tag doesn't have any specific attributes; it only uses global HTML attributes.

Browser Compatibility: The `<pre>` element is widely supported across all major browsers.

Accessibility Considerations: If used to display code, consider accompanying `<pre>` with the `<code>` element and potentially also a `role="doc-code"` ARIA role to enhance screen reader interpretation.

`<progress>`

Definition: The `<progress>` HTML element displays an indicator showing the completion progress of a task, typically displayed as a progress bar.

Usage: It's used when you want to indicate how much of a task has been completed, such as file upload progress.

Code Example:

```
<progress value="70" max="100"></progress>
```

Attributes
`value`: This attribute specifies how much of the task has been completed. - `max`: This attribute describes how much work the task requires in total.

Browser Compatibility: The `<progress>` element is widely supported across all major browsers.

Accessibility Considerations: The `<progress>` element is built with accessibility in mind and is accessible by default. Always specify both the `max` and `value` attributes for clear communication to assistive technologies.

`<q>`

Definition: The `<q>` HTML element represents a short inline quotation.

Usage: It's used when you want to indicate a short quotation that is inline with the surrounding text.

Code Example:

```
<p>Here is a <q>short quotation</q> in a senten
ce.</p>
```

Attributes
`cite`: Specifies the source URL or the attribution of the quotation.

Browser Compatibility: The `<q>` element is widely supported across all major browsers.

Accessibility Considerations: There are no specific accessibility considerations for the `<q>` tag.

This concludes the list of HTML tags that begin with "Q".

‹rb›

Definition: The ‹rb› HTML element represents the base text component of a ruby annotation, used to provide annotations for East Asian typography.

Usage: It's used in conjunction with the ‹ruby› element to define the base text component of a ruby annotation.

Code Example:

```
<ruby>
   <rb>漢</rb>
   <rp>(</rp>
   <rt>かん</rt>
   <rp>)</rp>
</ruby>
```

Attributes
This tag doesn't have any specific attributes; it only uses global HTML attributes.

Browser Compatibility: The ‹rb› element is supported by most modern browsers, but it has limited support in some older browsers.

Accessibility Considerations: The <rb> element is primarily used in East Asian typography and may not have specific accessibility considerations for general usage.

<rp>

Definition: The <rp> HTML element is used to provide parentheses around the fallback content for browsers that do not support ruby annotations.

Usage: It's used in conjunction with the <ruby> element to provide parentheses for the fallback content when ruby annotations are not supported.

Code Example:

```
<ruby>
   <rb>漢</rb>
   <rp>(</rp>
   <rt>かん</rt>
   <rp>)</rp>
</ruby>
```

Attributes
This tag doesn't have any specific attributes; it only uses global HTML attributes.

Browser Compatibility: The <rp> element is widely supported across all major browsers.

Accessibility Considerations: The <rp> element is primarily used in East Asian typography and may not have specific accessibility considerations for general usage.

<rt>

Definition: The <rt> HTML element represents the pronunciation of the characters that make up the base text component of a ruby annotation, used to provide annotations for East Asian typography.

Usage: It's used in conjunction with the <ruby> element to define the pronunciation component of a ruby annotation.

Code Example:

```
<ruby>
   <rb>漢</rb>
   <rp>(</rp>
   <rt>かん</rt>
   <rp>)</rp>
</ruby>
```

Attributes
This tag doesn't have any specific attributes; it only uses global HTML attributes.

Browser Compatibility: The <rt> element is supported by most modern browsers, but it has limited support in some older browsers.

Accessibility Considerations: The <rt> element is primarily used in East Asian typography and may not have specific accessibility considerations for general usage.

<rtc>

Definition: The <rtc> HTML element represents a ruby text container used to group the components of a ruby annotation.

Usage: It's used as a wrapper around the `<ruby>` element to group the base text, ruby text, and parentheses components of a ruby annotation.

Code Example:

```
<rtc>
  <ruby>
    <rb>漢</rb>
    <rp>(</rp>
    <rt>かん</rt>
    <rp>)</rp>
  </ruby>
  <ruby>
    <rb>字</rb>
    <rp>(</rp>
    <rt>じ</rt>
    <rp>)</rp>
  </ruby>
</rtc>
```

Attributes
This tag doesn't have any specific attributes; it only uses global HTML attributes.

Browser Compatibility: The `<rtc>` element has limited support in most browsers, especially older ones. It's primarily used in East Asian typography.

Accessibility Considerations: The element is primarily used in East Asian typography and may not have specific accessibility considerations for general usage.

`<ruby>`

Definition: The `<ruby>` HTML element represents a ruby annotation, used to provide pronunciation or other annotations for East Asian typography.

Usage: It's used to define a ruby annotation, which typically consists of a base text component and a ruby text component.

Code Example:

```
<ruby>
<rb>漢</rb>
<rp>(</rp>
<rt>かん</rt>
<rp>)</rp>
</ruby>
```

Attributes
This tag doesn't have any specific attributes; it only uses global HTML attributes.

Browser Compatibility: The <ruby> element is supported by most modern browsers, but it has limited support in some older browsers.

Accessibility Considerations: The <ruby> element is primarily used in East Asian typography and may not have specific accessibility considerations for general usage.

‹s›

Definition: The ‹s› HTML element represents content that is no longer accurate, relevant, or necessary to display. It is typically rendered with a strikethrough style.

Usage: It's used to indicate content that is no longer valid or should be disregarded.

Code Example:

```
<p><s>This information is no longer accurate.</s></p>
```

Attributes
This tag doesn't have any specific attributes; it only uses global HTML attributes.

Browser Compatibility: The ‹s› element is widely supported across all major browsers.

Accessibility Considerations: The ‹s› element may affect the visual presentation of the content but doesn't have direct accessibility considerations.

`<samp>`

Definition: The `<samp>` HTML element represents sample or quoted output from a computer program.

Usage: It's used to denote sample output or quoted content from a program.

Code Example:

```
<p>The command <samp>print("Hello, world!")</samp> displays a message.</p>
```

Attributes
This tag doesn't have any specific attributes; it only uses global HTML attributes.

Browser Compatibility: The `<samp>` element is widely supported across all major browsers.

Accessibility Considerations: The `<samp>` element doesn't have specific accessibility considerations, but it's important to provide alternative text or context for the sample output when necessary.

`<script>`

Definition: The `<script>` HTML element is used to embed or reference executable code, typically JavaScript, within an HTML document.

Usage: It's used to include or reference client-side scripts in an HTML page.

Code Example:

```
<script>
  function sayHello() {
    alert("Hello, world!");
```

```
  }
</script>
```

Attributes
src: Specifies the URL of an external script file.

type: Specifies the MIME type of the script. Default value is text/javascript.

Browser Compatibility: The <script> element is widely supported across all major browsers.

Accessibility Considerations: Ensure that any script-based functionality provided by the <script> element is accessible to users who rely on assistive technologies. Provide alternative content or fallback mechanisms for users who have disabled JavaScript.

<section>

Definition: The <section> HTML element represents a standalone section of a document, which is intended to be independently distributable or reusable.

Usage: It's used to mark up a semantically and contextually distinct section of content within a document.

Code Example:

```
<section>
  <h2>About Us</h2>
  <p>We are a company dedicated to providing qu
ality products.</p>
</section>
```

Attributes
This tag doesn't have any specific attributes; it only uses global HTML attributes.

Browser Compatibility: The `<section>` element is widely supported across all major browsers.

Accessibility Considerations: Use the `<section>` element to help provide structure and organize the content within a document. Ensure that the purpose and role of each section are clearly conveyed to assistive technologies.

`<select>`

Definition: The `<select>` HTML element represents a control that presents a menu of options, from which a user can select one or more.

Usage: It's used to create a dropdown list or a list box control.

Code Example:

```
<select>
  <option value="volvo">Volvo</option>
  <option value="saab">Saab</option>
  <option value="mercedes">Mercedes</option>
  <option value="audi">Audi</option>
</select>
```

Attributes:
`disabled`: If this Boolean attribute is present, the select element is disabled and cannot be interacted with.

`multiple`: If this Boolean attribute is present, multiple options can be selected.

`size`: Specifies the number of visible options in the dropdown list.

Browser Compatibility: The `<select>` element is widely supported across all major browsers.

Accessibility Considerations: When using the `<select>` element, provide clear labels and consider providing additional instructions or alternative methods for selecting options for users who rely on assistive technologies.

`<source>`

Definition: The `<source>` HTML element specifies multiple media resources for the `<video>`, `<audio>`, and `<picture>` elements.

Usage: It's used to provide multiple media sources for a media element, allowing the browser to choose the most suitable one.

Code Example:

```
<video controls>
  <source src="video.mp4" type="video/mp4">
  <source src="video.webm" type="video/webm">
  Your browser does not support the video tag.
</video>
```

Attributes
`src`: Specifies the URL of the media resource.

`type`: Specifies the MIME type of the media resource.

Browser Compatibility: The `<source>` element is widely supported across all major browsers.

Accessibility Considerations: When using the `<source>` element, ensure that alternative content or a fallback mechanism is provided for users who cannot access or play the media.

`<table>`

Definition: The `<table>` HTML element represents tabular data — that is, information presented in a two-dimensional table comprised of rows and columns.

Usage: It's used to create a table to organize and display data in a structured format.

Code Example:

```
<table>
  <tr>
    <th>Header 1</th>
    <th>Header 2</th>
  </tr>
  <tr>
    <td>Data 1</td>
    <td>Data 2</td>
  </tr>
</table>
```

Attributes
This tag doesn't have any specific attributes; it only uses global HTML attributes.

Browser Compatibility: The <table> element is widely supported across all major browsers.

Accessibility Considerations: When using tables, ensure appropriate markup is used to associate headers with cells, and provide alternative text or summaries for complex tables.

<tbody>

Definition: The <tbody> HTML element represents a block of rows in a table, which are grouped together for styling, scripting, or other purposes.

Usage: It's used to group a set of table rows within the <table> element.

Code Example:

```
<table>
<tbody>
    <tr>
        <td>Data 1</td>
    </tr>
    <tr>
        <td>Data 2</td>
    </tr>
</tbody>
</table>
```

Attributes
This tag doesn't have any specific attributes; it only uses global HTML attributes.

Browser Compatibility: The `<tbody>` element is widely supported across all major browsers.

Accessibility Considerations: Use appropriate table structure and labeling techniques to ensure that screen readers and other assistive technologies interpret the table content correctly.

`<td>`

Definition: The `<td>` HTML element represents a data cell within a table row.

Usage: It's used to define individual cells in a table, containing data or content.

Code Example:

```
<table>
  <tr>
    <td>Data 1</td>
    <td>Data 2</td>
  </tr>
</table>
```

Attributes
This tag doesn't have any specific attributes; it only uses global HTML attributes.

Browser Compatibility: The `<td>` element is widely supported across all major browsers.

Accessibility Considerations: Ensure that table cells are associated with appropriate headers using the `headers` attribute or `<th>` elements for better accessibility.

`<textarea>`

Definition: The `<textarea>` HTML element represents a multi-line plain-text editing control.

Usage: It's used to create a text input area where users can enter multiple lines of text.

Code Example:

```
<textarea rows="4" cols="50">
This is a multi-line text area.
</textarea>
```

Attributes

`rows`: Specifies the visible number of lines in the textarea.

`cols`: Specifies the visible width of the textarea (in characters).

Browser Compatibility: The `<textarea>` element is widely supported across all major browsers.

Accessibility Considerations: Provide a clear label and consider resizable and resizable options for better accessibility and user experience.

`<tfoot>`

Definition: The `<tfoot>` HTML element represents a block of footer content in a table, which provides additional information or summary for the table data.

Usage: It's used to group a set of table rows that contain footer content within the `<table>` element.

Code Example:

```
<table>
  <tfoot>
    <tr>
      <td>Footer 1</td>
    </tr>
    <tr>
      <td>Footer 2</td>
    </tr>
  </tfoot>
</table>
```

Attributes
This tag doesn't have any specific attributes; it only uses global HTML attributes.

Browser Compatibility: The <tfoot> element is widely supported across all major browsers.

Accessibility Considerations: Use appropriate table structure and labeling techniques to ensure that screen readers and other assistive technologies interpret the table footer content correctly.

<th>

Definition: The <th> HTML element represents a header cell within a table row, which provides context or labels for the associated data cells.

Usage: It's used to define header cells in a table, typically placed within the <thead> or <tfoot> section.

Code Example:

```
<table>
  <thead>
    <tr>
      <th>Header 1</th>
      <th>Header 2</th>
```

```
    </tr>
  </thead>
  <tbody>
    <tr>
      <td>Data 1</td>
      <td>Data 2</td>
    </tr>
  </tbody>
</table>
```

Attributes

This tag doesn't have any specific attributes; it only uses global HTML attributes.

Browser Compatibility: The <th> element is widely supported across all major browsers.

Accessibility Considerations: Use <th> elements to provide clear and accessible header labels for data cells within a table.

<thead>

Definition: The <thead> HTML element represents a block of header content in a table, which groups the header rows together.

Usage: It's used to group a set of table rows that contain header content within the <table> element.

Code Example:

```
<table>
  <thead>
    <tr>
      <th>Header 1</th>
      <th>Header 2</th>
    </tr>
  </thead>
```

```
  <tbody>
    <tr>
      <td>Data 1</td>
      <td>Data 2</td>
    </tr>
  </tbody>
</table>
```

Attributes
This tag doesn't have any specific attributes; it only uses global HTML attributes.

Browser Compatibility: The `<thead>` element is widely supported across all major browsers.

Accessibility Considerations: Use appropriate table structure and labeling techniques to ensure that screen readers and other assistive technologies interpret the table header content correctly.

`<time>`

Definition: The `<time>` HTML element represents either a specific point in time or a duration.

Usage: It's used to mark up dates, times, or durations in a machine-readable format.

Code Example:

```
<p>Published on <time datetime="2023-06-30">June 30, 2023</time></p>
```

Attributes
`datetime`: Specifies the date, time, or duration in a machine-readable format.

Browser Compatibility: The `<time>` element is widely supported across all major browsers.

Accessibility Considerations: Ensure that the content within the `<time>` element is also presented in a human-readable format for better accessibility.

<ul>

Definition: The <ul> HTML element represents an unordered list of items.

Usage: It's used to create a bulleted list where the order of the items doesn't matter.

Code Example:

```
<ul>
   <li>Item 1</li>
   <li>Item 2</li>
   <li>Item 3</li>
</ul>
```

Attributes
This tag doesn't have any specific attributes; it only uses global HTML attributes.

Browser Compatibility: The <ul> element is widely supported across all major browsers.

Accessibility Considerations: Ensure that the content within the <ul> element is structured and labeled properly for screen readers and other assistive technologies.

`<u>`

Definition: The `<u>` HTML element represents text that should be stylistically rendered with an underline.

Usage: It's used to indicate text that should be visually underlined.

Code Example:

```
<p>This is an <u>underlined</u> text.</p>
```

Attributes
This tag doesn't have any specific attributes; it only uses global HTML attributes.

Browser Compatibility: The `<u>` element is widely supported across all major browsers.

Accessibility Considerations: Avoid using the `<u>` element solely for stylistic purposes, as underlines can sometimes be associated with hyperlinks. Ensure that the underline doesn't cause confusion for users.

`<var>`

Definition: The `<var>` HTML element represents the name of a variable or placeholder text.

Usage: It's used to mark up variables or placeholders within the context of computer programming or mathematics.

Code Example:

```
<p>The value of <var>x</var> is 10.</p>
```

Attributes
This tag doesn't have any specific attributes; it only uses global HTML attributes.

Browser Compatibility: The `<var>` element is widely supported across all major browsers.

Accessibility Considerations: Ensure that the meaning and context of variables marked with the `<var>` element are clear to users who rely on assistive technologies.

<video>

Definition: The <video> HTML element is used to embed or playback video content within an HTML document.

Usage: It's used to include video content in a web page.

Code Example:

```
<video controls>
  <source src="video.mp4" type="video/mp4">
  <source src="video.webm" type="video/webm">
  Your browser does not support the video tag.
</video>
```

Attributes

src: Specifies the URL of the video file.

controls: Adds video controls, such as play, pause, and volume.

autoplay: Specifies that the video should start playing automatically.

loop: Specifies that the video should loop back to the beginning when it reaches the end.

muted: Specifies that the video's audio should be muted by default.

Browser Compatibility: The <video> element is widely supported across all major browsers.

Accessibility Considerations: Ensure that alternative content or captions are provided for users who cannot access or play the video.

`<wbr>`

Definition: The `<wbr>` HTML element represents a word break opportunity, indicating where a word can be divided when line-wrapping occurs.

Usage: It's used to suggest a potential line break within a word.

Code Example:

```
<p>This is a longword\<wbr>that can be line-wra
pped.</p>
```

Attributes
This tag doesn't have any specific attributes; it only uses global HTML attributes.

Browser Compatibility: The `<wbr>` element is widely supported across all major browsers.

Accessibility Considerations: The `<wbr>` element doesn't have specific accessibility considerations. Ensure that the line break suggestion doesn't affect the readability or comprehension of the content.

<webview>

Definition: The <webview> HTML element is used to embed web content within an application or extension.

Usage: It's primarily used in platform-specific applications or extensions to display web-based content.

Code Example:

```
<webview src="https://www.example.com"></webview>
```

Attributes
src: Specifies the URL of the web content to be displayed.

Browser Compatibility: The <webview> element is not widely supported as it is primarily used in platform-specific applications or extensions.

Accessibility Considerations: The accessibility of content within the <webview> element depends on the platform or application context in which it is used. Follow platform-specific guidelines for ensuring accessibility in such cases.

<xmp>

Definition: The <xmp> HTML element represents a block of preformatted text, preserving white spaces and line breaks.

Usage: It's used to display code or other text content exactly as it is, without any interpretation or processing.

Code Example:

```
<xmp>
  <p>This is a paragraph.</p>
  <ul>
    <li>Item 1</li>
    <li>Item 2</li>
  </ul>
</xmp>
```

Attributes

This tag doesn't have any specific attributes; it only uses global HTML attributes.

Browser Compatibility: The <xmp> element is not widely supported as it has been deprecated. It is recommended to use CSS for styling preformatted text.

Accessibility Considerations: The <xmp> element doesn't have specific accessibility considerations. Ensure that the content within it is still readable and understandable for all users.

<xml>

Definition: The <xml> HTML element is used to include or embed XML content within an HTML document.

Usage: It's used to incorporate XML content into an HTML page.

Code Example:

```
<xml version="1.0">
  <root>
    <element>Content</element>
  </root>
</xml>
```

Attributes

This tag doesn't have any specific attributes; it only uses global HTML attributes.

Browser Compatibility: The <xml> element is not widely supported as it has been deprecated. It is recommended to use other techniques, such as AJAX or JavaScript, to work with XML content.

Accessibility Considerations: The accessibility of content within the <xml> element depends on how it is handled and presented within the HTML document.

Ensure that the XML content is accessible and understandable to all users.

Global HTML Attributes

Global HTML attributes are attributes that can be used on any HTML element.

Usage

Global attributes offer additional information or controls over the element they are added to. They can be used for various purposes such as providing tooltips, setting an element's language, defining whether an element is editable, associating data with an element, and so on.

Attributes Table

Attribute	Purpose	Possible Values	Usage Example
accesskey	Specifies a shortcut key to activate/focus an element.	Any single character.	`<button accesskey="p">Press</button>`
class	Specifies one or more classnames for an element.	Any text string.	`<p class="highlight">This is a highlighted paragraph.</p>`
contenteditable	Specifies whether the content of an element is editable or not.	true, false, inherit	`<p contenteditable="true">This paragraph is editable. Click here to edit this text.</p>`
data-*	Used to store custom data private to the page or application.	Any text string.	`<p data-custom="customValue">This paragraph contains custom data.</p>`
dir	Specifies the text direction for the content in an element.	ltr (left-to-right), rtl (right-to-left), auto	`<p dir="rtl">This is a paragraph with 'right-to-left' text direction.</p>`
hidden	Specifies that an element is not yet, or is no longer, relevant.	None (boolean attribute).	`<p hidden>This paragraph is not shown.</p>`
id	Specifies a unique id for an element.	Any text string.	`<p id="intro">This is the introduction paragraph.</p>`

Attribute	Purpose	Possible Values	Usage Example
lang	Specifies the language of the element's content.	Any valid language code.	`<p lang="es">Este es un párrafo en español.</p>`
style	Specifies inline CSS style for an element.	Any valid CSS.	`<p style="color:red;">This is a red paragraph.</p>`
tabindex	Specifies the tabbing order of an element.	Any positive integer.	`<input tabindex="1" type="text">`
title	Adds extra information about an element. The information is shown as a tooltip when the mouse hovers over the element.	Any text string.	`<p title="This is a tooltip">Hover over me.</p>`

www.ingramcontent.com/pod-product-compliance
Lightning Source LLC
La Vergne TN
LVHW051743050326
832903LV00029B/2700